My Jungle Quilt

Pattern and Instructions

Summerside Lane
Stories and Quilts for Children

Acknowledgements

I wish to thank all my family, friends and neighbors who have supported me and helped me during this project. Particularly, I wish to thank my son David for his advice, teaching and design expertise, my daughter Jackie for her artistic suggestions and my husband Norman for his constant encouragement. I am indebted to the people who have tried the pattern and given their advice: Donna Martiniak and Colette Schneider. I am truly grateful to those who patiently edited this work: David Burnett, Lynn Yeo and Colette Schneider.

I have been taken on this journey by the enthusiasm of those families who have enjoyed the quilts and their darling children: Elise, Charlie, Laura, Sofie, Peyton and Braedon.

Contents

List of Diagrams

Introduction

Here is a quilt for you to make and a storybook for you to share with that special little one you know. When you have finished your quilt you can personalize the storybook by taking a photograph of your quilt and putting it in the book.

There are plenty of options open to you as you make the quilt. You can embellish the quilt with extra embroidery and quilting or you can keep it very simple. Whatever your quilting skill level and however you finish the quilt, the storybook will go with it.

The storybook is sure to delight and capture the imagination of the little one as he or she snuggles in this lovely quilt made by you.

Jenifer Burnett

My Jungle Quilt

Pattern and Instructions

Please read through all instructions before commencing your quilt.

Approximate Quilt Sizes: **Baby Quilt   34" x 45"**
                           Child's Quilt   43" x 56"

Basic Equipment

Sewing machine
Walking foot attachment for machine quilting (optional)
Needles: assorted sizes for embroidery, appliqué, quilting and machine
Scissors: various, including small sharp pointed scissors for cutting out
  and clipping the appliqué pieces
Rotary cutter and cutting board
Machine threads, embroidery thread (as listed below) and quilting
  thread.   Note: nylon thread is not recommended for baby quilts
9 1/2" square or larger ruler
Chalk or washable marking pencil
Template plastic or freezer paper
Fusible web for machine appliqué
Masking tape
Stabilizer (optional)

Baby Quilt Shopping List
and Fabric Guide

Fabric Requirements (100% cotton recommended)

Background blocks*   **1 yd.** or
                                  12 x 9½" squares

> *Note: 1/3 yd. of fabric will make four background blocks or a fat quarter will give
> you 2 blocks per quarter. Background blocks may be made in a variety of colors.

Appliqué figures (12)   **Remnants** see template patterns,
                                  use blue and green fabric for parrot

Fusible web   **1¼ yd.** machine appliqué only
Sashing   **3/4 yd.**
Binding   **2/3 yd.**
Backing   **1½ yd.**
Batting   **37" x 47"** use thin, washable batting for
                                  hand or machine quilting

Embroidery Floss

Dark brown (monkey, leopard)   Dark blue (parrot)
Medium brown (lion, giraffe)   Yellow (leopard, lion and parrot)
Green (crocodile)
Black (elephant, buffalo, hippopotamus, flamingo, zebra, ostrich)

Baby Quilt Fabric Guide

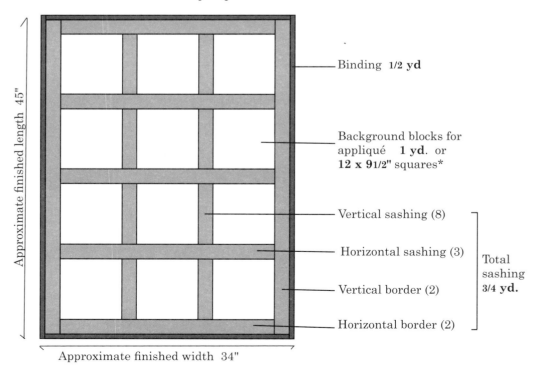

Approximate finished length 45"

Binding **1/2 yd**

Background blocks for
appliqué **1 yd.** or
12 x 9½" squares*

Vertical sashing (8)

Horizontal sashing (3)

Vertical border (2)

Horizontal border (2)

Total
sashing
3/4 yd.

Approximate finished width 34"

Child's Quilt Shopping List
and Fabric Guide

Fabric Requirements (100% cotton recommended)

Background blocks*	**1 yd. or** **12 x 9**1/2**" squares**

   *Note: 1/3 yd. of fabric will make four background blocks or a fat quarter will give you 2 blocks per quarter. Background blocks may be made in a variety of colors.

Appliqué figures (12)	**Remnants** see template patterns, use blue and green fabric for parrot
Fusible web	**1**1/4 **yd.** machine appliqué only
Frames for appliqué blocks	1/2 **yd.**
Sashing	**1 yd.**
Outer border	3/4 **yd.** use extra for directional fabric
Binding	2/3 **yd.**
Backing*	**2**3/8 **yd.** twice width of quilt top **or** **3**1/8 **yd.** twice length of quilt top if fabric is directional
Batting	**46" x 57"** use thin, washable batting for machine or hand quilting

Embroidery Floss

Dark brown (monkey, leopard)   Dark blue (parrot)
Medium brown (lion, giraffe)   Yellow (leopard, lion, parrot)
Green (crocodile)
Black (elephant, buffalo, hippopotamus, flamingo, zebra, ostrich)

   *For non directional fabric, cut two lengths the same measurement as the width of the quilt top + 3" and sew together lengthwise. For directional fabric, cut two lengths the same measurement as the length of the quilt + 3" and sew together lengthwise as shown in the Backing Guide p. 10.

Child's Quilt Fabric Guide

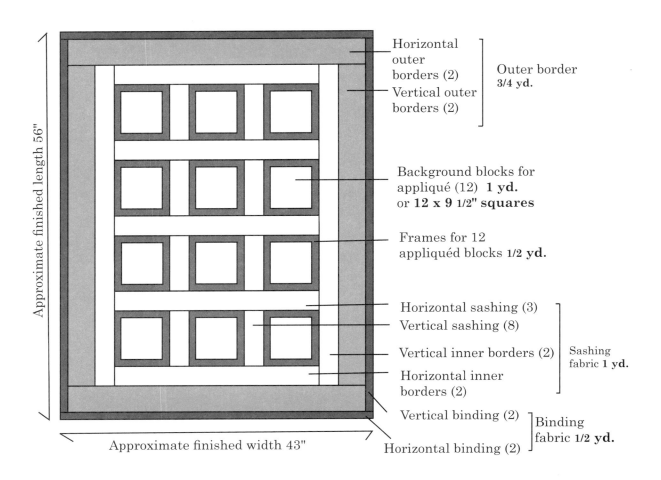

Approximate finished length 56"

Approximate finished width 43"

Horizontal outer borders (2)
Vertical outer borders (2)
Outer border 3/4 yd.

Background blocks for appliqué (12) **1 yd.**
or **12 x 9 1/2" squares**

Frames for 12 appliquéd blocks **1/2 yd.**

Horizontal sashing (3)
Vertical sashing (8)
Vertical inner borders (2)
Horizontal inner borders (2)
Sashing fabric **1 yd.**

Vertical binding (2)
Horizontal binding (2)
Binding fabric **1/2 yd.**

Backing Guide for Child's Quilt

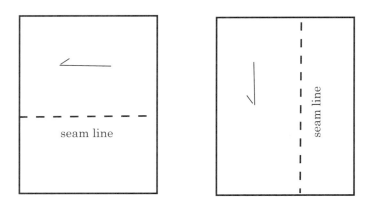

seam line

seam line

Instructions for Both Quilts

Background Blocks

Cut twelve 9½" squares of background fabric using the ruler, cutter and mat.

Layout

To decide which appliqué pieces go with which background blocks, it is helpful to **lay out** all the 9½" blocks at this point to see where each will go in relation to the other. The background fabric color will make a difference in your decision. Also the orientation of each animal is important as the animals look best facing straight ahead or in towards the center blocks, rather than outwards towards the edges of the quilt. Once the orientation and the positioning have been decided, keep a record of the order and colors, e.g., buffalo on yellow, zebra on brown. **Draw a diagram of your planned layout.**

Appliqué Figures

Prepare the figures for machine appliqué

Follow the instructions given with the chosen bonding or stabilizing product and use the enclosed template patterns to **cut out** the appliqué figures that go on the background blocks. **Mark** the embroidery lines.

Prepare the figures for hand appliqué

Use the enclosed template patterns to prepare the figures to be appliquéd on the background blocks. **Place** the template plastic or freezer paper over each pattern, **trace** the outline and **mark** embroidery lines. **Cut out** the templates. **Place** the templates onto the right side of the fabric remnants and **outline** the figures with chalk or washable marking pencil. If using freezer paper, **iron** on freezer paper templates onto the right side of the fabric. **Cut** the figures out with **a 3/16" turn-under allowance. Clip all curves.**

Sew on the appliqué

Center the figures onto each of the background blocks. If you have pieces that have turn-unders, allow for this. If you are using a bonding agent to hold the appliqué pieces onto the background fabric, follow the manufacturer's instructions at this time. Otherwise, **pin or baste** all the appliqué pieces to each background block. **Sew** in place, using your favorite appliqué method by machine or by hand.

Embroider details onto each figure in outline stitch or satin stitch. See **Diagram 1, p. 12**. Use the templates and pictures in the **story book** as a guide.

Add any **extra embroidery** embellishments or **extra appliqué** at this time.

Diagram 1
Embroidery Stitches

Satin Stitch   Outline Stitch

Piecing the Quilt Tops

Your blocks are now ready to piece together with sashes. For the Baby Quilt follow the directions below and for the Child's Quilt turn to p. 15.

Quilt Top Assembly
Baby Quilt

Plan to join the blocks together with three blocks across the top and four down according to your original outline. **Check** the orientation and overall effect.

Sashing

Cut 9 strips of sashing fabric **2" x 42"**. **Cut 8** pieces **2" x 9½"** from these strips. **Join** this sashing to the appliquéd blocks, using ¼" seams as shown in **Diagram 2, Steps 1 - 3, p. 13**. Press each seam away from the appliquéd blocks. **Measure** the width of each pieced section and make sure they all match each other. The width of each section at the end of Step 3 should measure **30½"**. If the sections are not equal, block the sections with an iron.

Diagram 2
Steps 1 - 3
Sashing for Baby Quilt

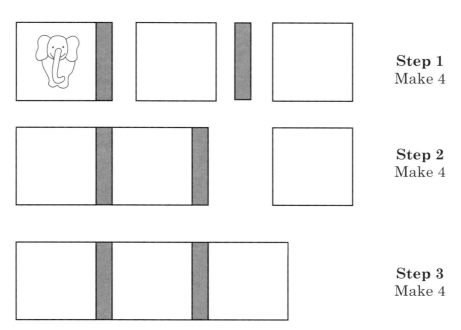

Cut 5 pieces from the sashing strips **2" x 30½"**. Join, with 1/4" seams, one width to each section as in **Diagram 2, Step 4, p. 14**. To join these horizontal sections, match the center of both the sash and the pieced section and pin them and then pin at both ends. This holds the pieces firmly and the pieced edge can be eased to fit the sash as you stitch.

Join the four sections together with 1/4" seams as in **Diagram 2, Step 5, p. 14**. Be sure to check their positions as set in your original outline. From the remaining strips, add bottom and side sashes (the vertical and horizontal borders); see **Diagram 2, Step 6, p. 14** and use the same method of matching and pinning as described above in Step 4. You may need to lengthen the side pieces by adding an extra piece from the leftover strips, that should be joined on the bias as in

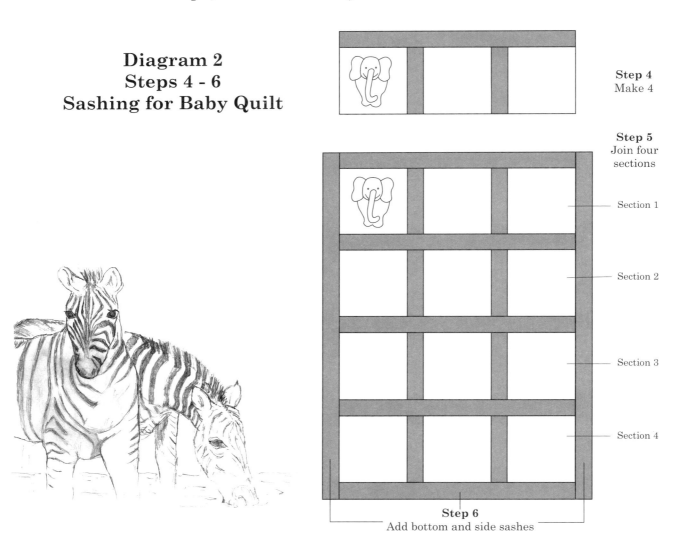

**Diagram 2
Steps 4 - 6
Sashing for Baby Quilt**

Step 4
Make 4

Step 5
Join four
sections

Section 1

Section 2

Section 3

Section 4

Step 6
Add bottom and side sashes

Diagram 3, p. 15.
Press the quilt top, both front and back, and make sure all seams on both sides of the quilt top lie as flat as possible.

Your quilt top is now ready to sandwich (layer) and quilt.
Turn to **Quilting Instructions, p. 19.**

Diagram 3
Joining on the Bias

Lay strips, right sides together, at right angles to each other, and stitch on the diagonal line as shown. Press open on both sides.

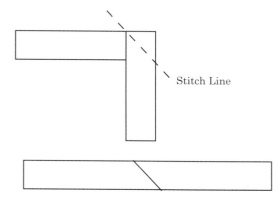

Stitch Line

Press seam open

Quilt Top Assembly
Child's Quilt Top

The Child's Quilt is pieced together with frames for each individual block and with sashing and an outer border.

Plan to join the blocks together with three blocks across the top and four down, according to your original outline. **Check** the orientation and overall effect.

Frame the appliquéd blocks

Cut 12 strips of **frame fabric 1" x 42"** to frame the appliquéd blocks.
Cut 2 strips **1" x 9½"** and **2** strips **1" x 10½"** from these pieces for each block. **Sew** one 9½" strip to each of the horizontal sides of the appliquéd blocks and **press** seams away from the center. **Sew** one 10½" strip to each of the vertical sides of the appliquéd blocks and **press** seams away from the center. Shown in **Diagram 4, p. 16.**

Diagram 4
Framing the Appliquéd Blocks

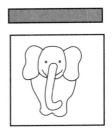   

Sashing

Cut 10 strips **2" x 42"** of **sashing fabric**. From these strips **cut 8** pieces **2" x 10½".** **Sew**, with ¼" seams, one piece to each of the blocks as shown in **Diagram 5, Steps 1- 3, p. 16**.

Measure the width of each pieced section and make sure they all match each other. The width of each pieced section should now measure **33½".** If the sections are not equal, block the sections with an iron.

Diagram 5
Steps 1- 3
Sashing for Child's Quilt

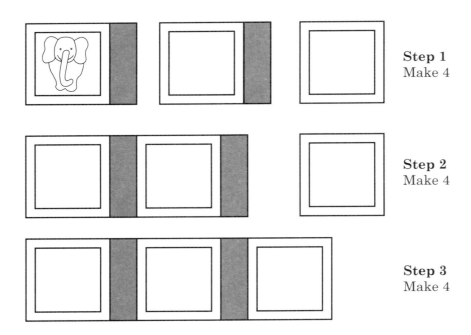

Step 1
Make 4

Step 2
Make 4

Step 3
Make 4

Sew the horizontal sashes with 1/4" seams to the pieced sections as in **Diagram 5, Step 4, p. 17**, matching the center of both the sash and the pieced section and pinning them. This holds the pieces firmly and the pieced edge can be eased to fit the sash as you stitch.

Check the positions as set in your original outline.

Diagram 5
Steps 4 - 6
Sashing for Child's Quilt

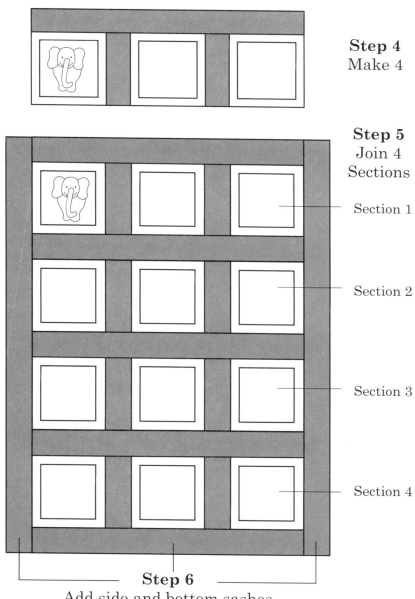

Step 4
Make 4

Step 5
Join 4
Sections

Section 1

Section 2

Section 3

Section 4

Step 6
Add side and bottom sashes

Join all four sections together with 1/4" seams as shown in **Diagram 5, Step 5, p. 17**.

From the remaining strips, add bottom and side sashes (the vertical and horizontal borders), see **Diagram 5, Step 6, p. 17**. You will need to join **extra strips** for the sides, joining the strips together with a bias seam shown in **Diagram 3, p. 15**.

Outer Border

Cut 6 strips **3 1/4" x 42"** from the outer border fabric. **Sew** with 1/4" seams, one of these strips to the top and one to the bottom of your quilt top as shown in **Diagram 6, p. 18**. **Trim excess.** Add one strip to each

Diagram 6
Outer Border for Child's Quilt

Step 1
Add horizontal borders (2)
(top and bottom)

Step 2
Add vertical borders (2)
(one on each side)

of the sides, which you will need to lengthen to fit by using extra from the strips and joining them with a bias seam as in **Diagram 3, p. 15**. **Trim excess.**

Press your quilt top on both sides and make sure all seams lie flat and that it is perfectly rectangular.

Quilting Instructions
Both Quilts

Measure the quilt top. **Prepare the backing** by cutting the backing fabric **3"** wider and longer than the quilt top (see the Backing Guide for the Child's Quilt on p. 10). **Prepare the batting** the same way with **3"** extra allowance to the quilt top measurements.

The quilt is now ready for layering by **sandwiching** the top, batting, and backing.

Sandwich the quilt
Lay out the **backing**, **wrong side up**, on a flat surface. Tape it down to keep it tight. Spread the **batting** on top of the backing, smoothing out all wrinkles. **Center** the **quilt top front side up** on top of the batting, leaving 1½" batting and backing as extra all around. To keep it from moving, tape it or weight it.

For **machine quilting**, **pin** the layers together every 6 inches. For **hand quilting**, **baste** layers together every 6-10 inches vertically and horizontally. As well baste diagonally, corner-to-corner, forming an "X" crossing in the center of the quilt. Remove tapes.

Quilting Instructions

Quilt by machine stitching in the seam line (ditch) around each appliquéd block using a walking foot (optional), or **hand quilt** as desired.

Outline the figures by **free motion machine quilting** or by **hand quilting**.

Any **extra quilting** may be done at this time.

Binding Instructions
Both quilts

You can finish the quilt by adding a binding using your favorite method or you can use the method described below which uses a double thickness of fabric.

Prepare the quilt by cutting away any excess batting and backing fabric, making sure the quilt is rectangular. **Press**, if necessary.

Cut 5 pieces of binding fabric **4" x 42"**. **Fold** each piece in half lengthwise and **press**. **Sew** the doubled binding strips, with 1/4" seams, **to the front of the quilt top, the raw edges matching**. Use the method described in the instructions for the **Outer Border p. 18**. **Press** and roll to the back of quilt. **Hand stitch in place and miter the corners.**

Finishing Touch

Personalize the accompanying storybook by placing a 4" x 6" photograph of your finished quilt on page 31 of the storybook opposite the final poem.

Sign and date your quilt.

You may make a personal label to sew on the quilt by following the instructions on page xvii of the Templates section.

Personal Notes

My Jungle Quilt

TEMPLATES

Light lines are the embroidery lines

Add extra **3/16"** around each figure
for turn-unders

Elephant Template

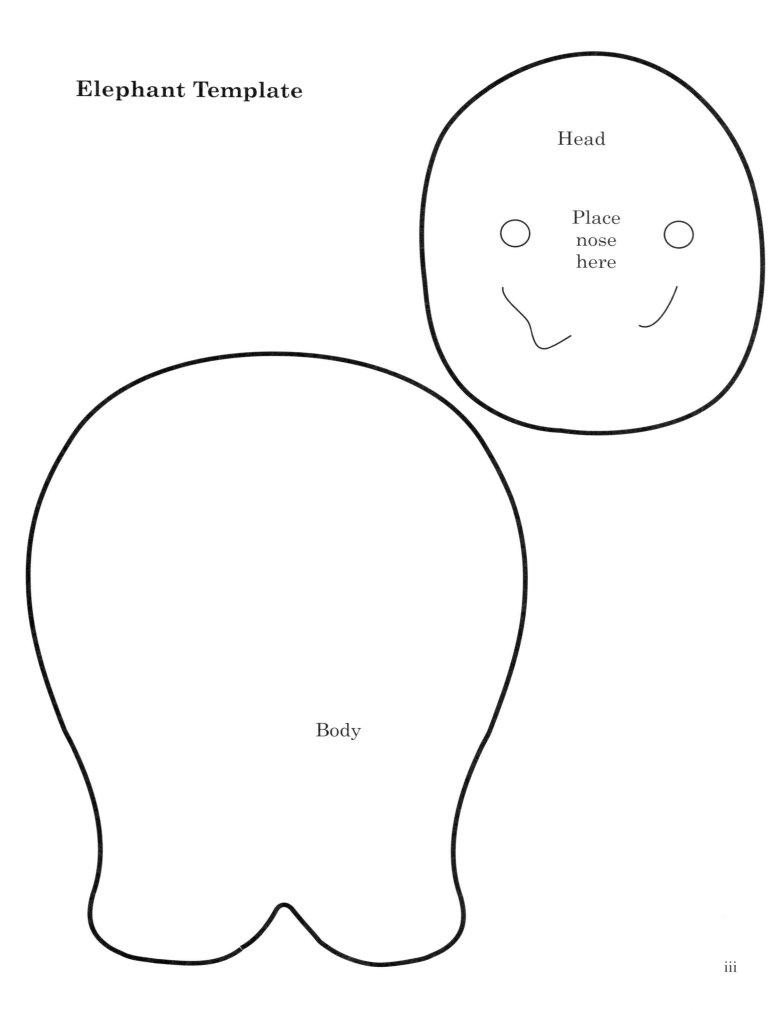

Head

Place
nose
here

Body

Elephant Template
Trunk and Ears

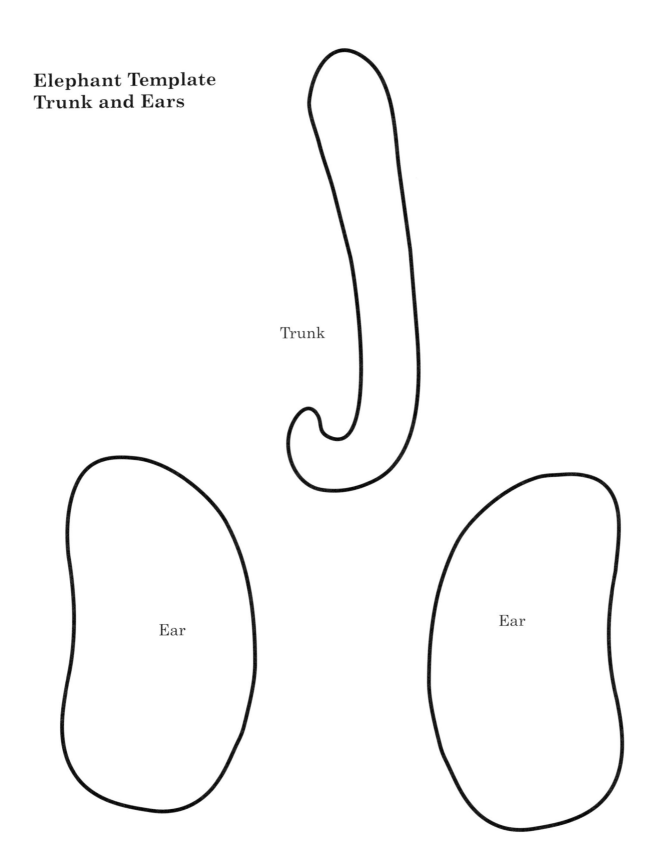

Trunk

Ear

Ear

Monkey Template

Monkey
Nose

Monkey
Ears

Buffalo Template

Lion Template

Lion Mane

Flamingo Template

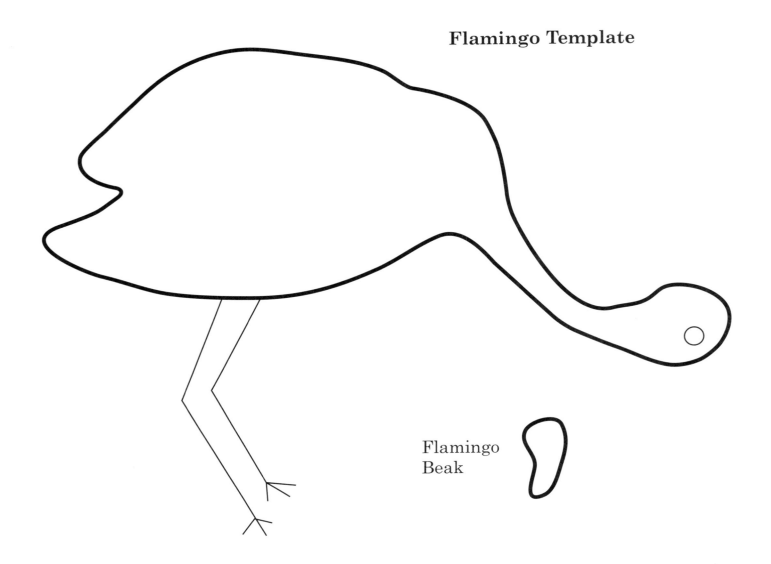

Flamingo
Beak

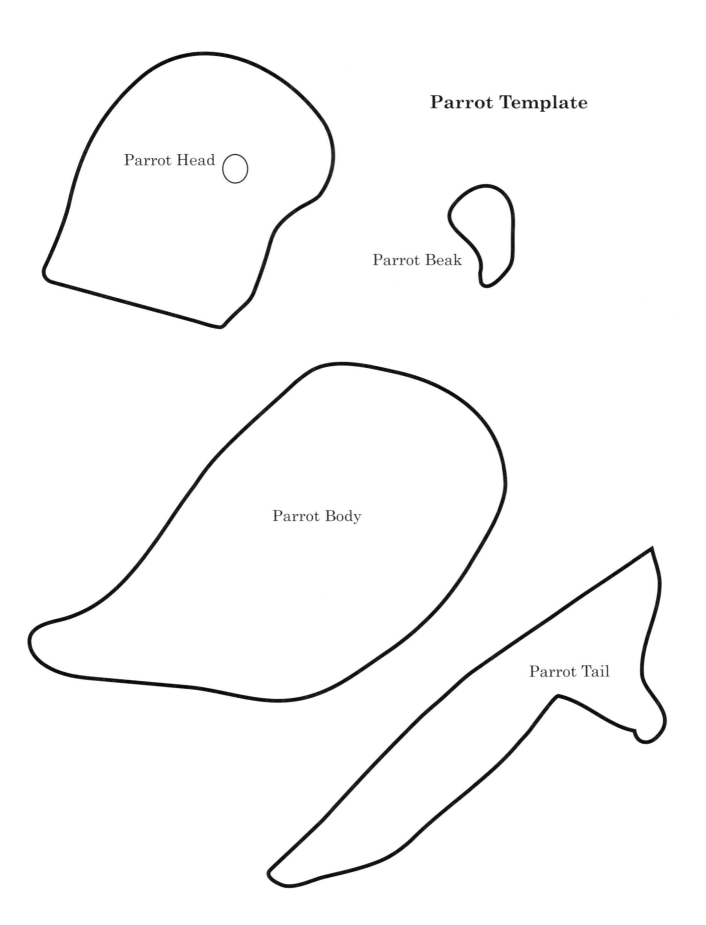

Parrot Head

Parrot Beak

Parrot Body

Parrot Tail

Parrot Template

Leaf and Branch Templates for
Giraffe Block and Parrot Block

Leaves for
Giraffe Block

Giraffe / Leaf
Cut three

Parrot / Leaf
Cut three

Branch and Leaves for
Parrot Block

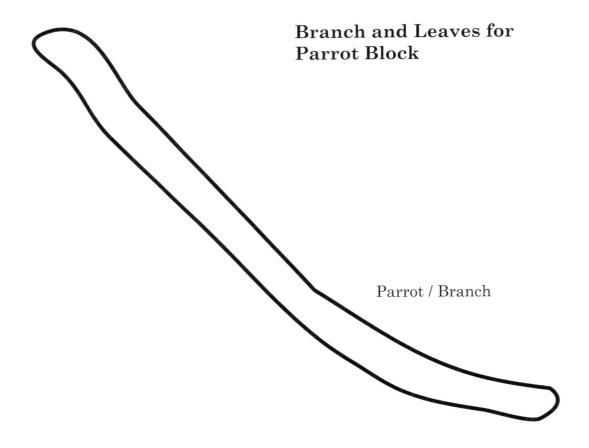

Parrot / Branch

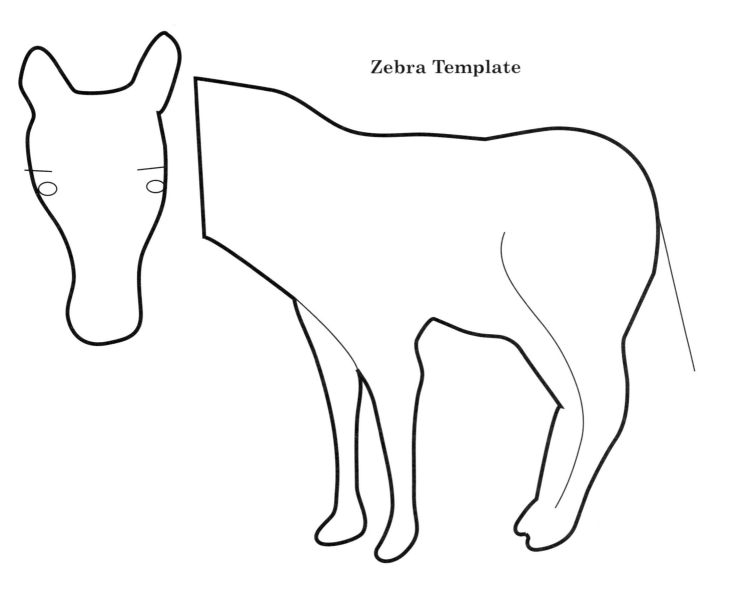

Zebra Template

Leopard Template

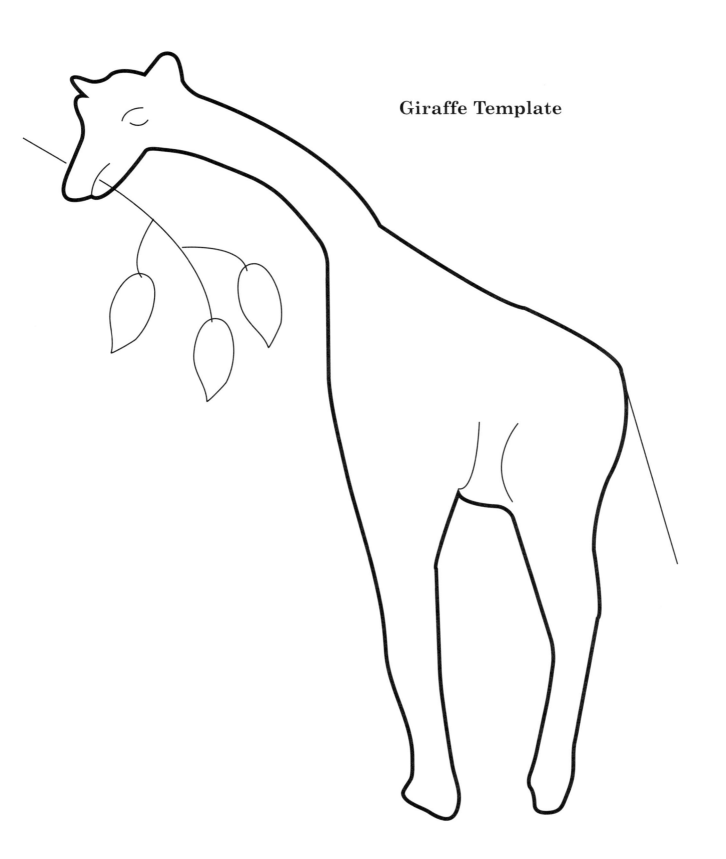

Giraffe Template

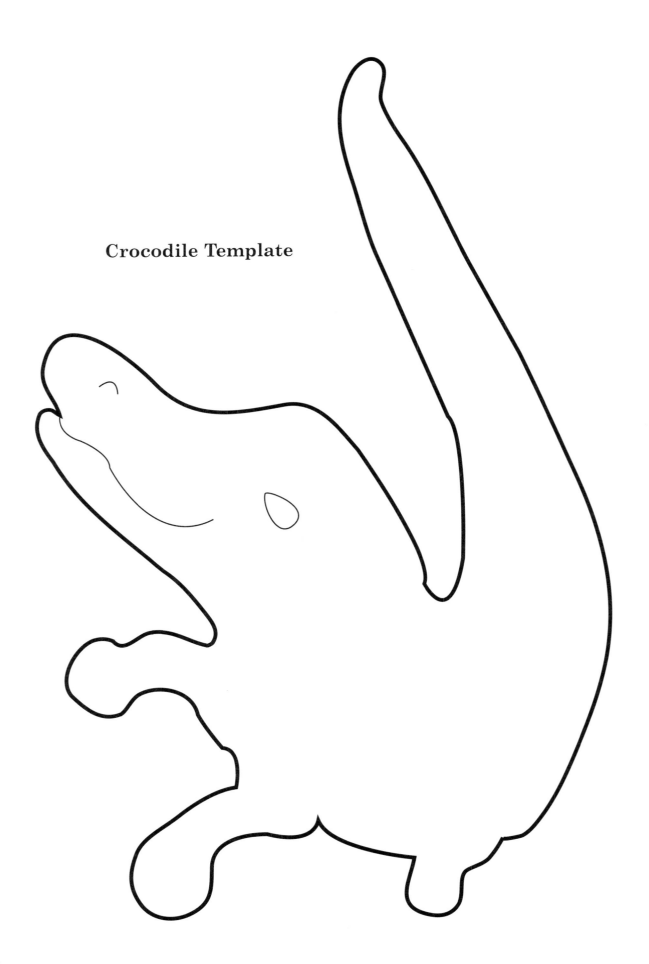

Crocodile Template

Ostrich Template

Hippopotamus Template

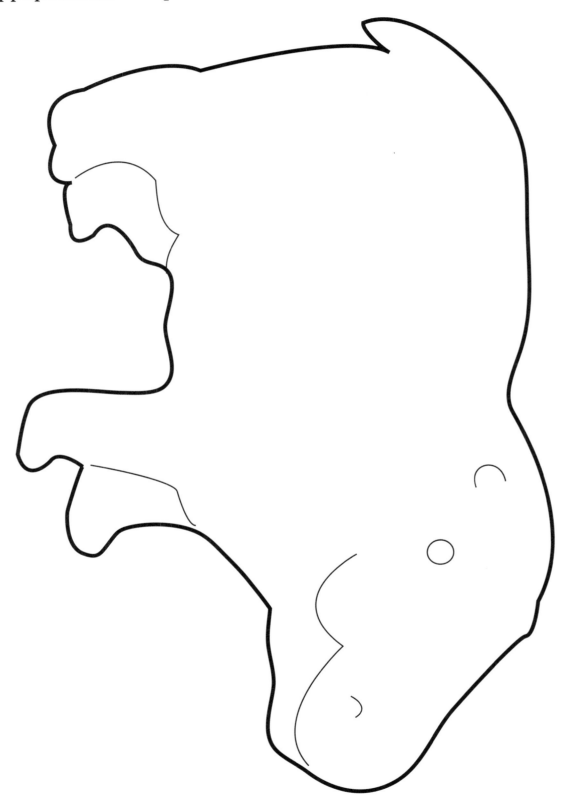

Personal Quilt Label

You may wish to make your own personal label. Either purchase pre-treated fabric in sheets with peel-off paper on the back or use fabric of your choice and purchase a fabric treatment to ready it for printing.

Copy the label below, fill in the details and add other information and scan it into your computer. Reduce the size of the label to your requirements and, using an ink jet printer, print this onto the prepared cloth. Follow the instructions for sealing the ink to prevent bleeding. Cut out the label and hand stitch it onto the back of the quilt.

Permission is hereby given to scan this label design and use it to attach to your quilt.

Jenifer Burnett introduces a series of stories and quilts for children.

This first pattern and the accompanying storybook, **My Jungle Quilt**, were inspired by memories of a safari to Africa.

Jenifer has been a quilter for over twenty years and has designed and taught quilting both in the USA and abroad. She was born in England, married an American and, after many years living in various states and overseas, has now retired to Vermont.

Summerside Lane derived its name from the Yorkshire side of the family in England.

Ordering Information

Patterns and the storybook, **My Jungle Quilt**, can be purchased at your local quilt store or on line at:

www.Summersidelane.com